Of Memories and Imaginings

Of Memories and Imaginings

Greg Willson

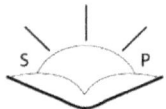

Of Memories and Imaginings by Greg Willson
ISBN 978-0-994-5990-2-5
Copyright © Greg Willson. All rights reserved.
First Published 2017 by Sunshine Press
Cover Design by James Hickey
Publication Production Services by Connie M. Berg

Dedication
To Thelma,
without whom the world,
especially my tiny part of it,
would be a darker, lesser place.

Acknowledgements
To Connie Berg,
with sincere thanks for the support and practical
assistance in taking this collection from an idea to reality.
To other members of the Paddocks Creative Writing Group:
Harriet; Brenda; Jeanette; Jan; Bob and Peter.
Their enthusiasm for the works encouraged
the compilation of this book.

Contents

Escaping Rest 1
A Hole in the World 2
New Year 3
Stolen 4
Winters of Longing 6
Children Who Fell to Doom 7
Shivering 8
Of Memories and Imaginings 9
Waiting Women 10
Riding the Dog 12
Last Request 13
Bakehouse 14
Reach for Stars 15
Yesterday and Tomorrow 16
Just Dreaming 17
Wind, Sea and Ship 18
In 1962 19
South 20
When We Are Gone 22
In My Mind 23
The Promise 24
Alone 25
Gravity 26
Christmas at Carrick Hill 28
Tribute Trees 29
Train Whispers 30
The Plant, the Town, the People 31
I'm Coming Home 32
Unfound Door 33
Thomas and Emily 34
Walk With Me 36

A Memory Lost	37
The Rising	38
Flying Kites on Sunday	39
Birthday Lottery	40
Country of Myself	42
Rotary Kids	43
The Port and the Container Terminal	44
Moonta 1873	46
The Arrival	47
Today	48
On Gazing at a Photograph of Myself as a Child	49
One Perfect Tree	50
M.V. Blythe Star	51
A Father's Sons	52
The Distance of Things	54
If I Could	55
Morning Soliloquy	56
I Could Have Been a Sailor	57
Rose and Son	58
He Who Never Tries	59
One House	60
Journey	62
The Writing and the Wronging	63
Once and Now	64
The Wondrous Purple Box	65
House on Mercer Street	66
I Am the Dreamer	67
Time-Out	68
Lady of the Night	69
Sleepy Warm	71

A poem is an open door
leading the reader to discover
what lies beyond.

Escaping Rest

Through the dozing pillowed dark,
All the workaday flock is sleeping,
And the rhythm of the breathing,
And the sounds of steady snoozing,
Gently numbers napping moments,
To time the passing of the night.

Now the grind and daily humdrum,
With its constant pushing pace,
And the ticking, tricking time clock,
With its frenzied onward chase,
Are tucked away and curled up snug,
Dulled and dormant in the still.

And slumber gives escaping rest,
And dreaming lightens heavy load.
And night it gaps the endless flow
Of unceasing drudge and toil,
Stretching, reaching forever and on,
To eternity's edge—then around again.

A Hole in the World

There's a hole in the world,
And I fear I'll slip it through,
As I scramble for finger-holds,
Fighting the push and the roar
Of others stumbling and sliding,
Arms flapping, legs kicking,
Towards, into and on down
This growing gape in the ground.

There's a thundering in the air,
So angry and affronting,
With its thumping, thudding, crashing,
As it drowns all the softer sounds
That bring clarity and calm,
Like the small appeal of reason,
And the long, pondering silence,
And the hushed library quiet.

There's a hurricane all about
With a rush so fully fierce,
As it pounds and it pushes,
Across, around and though
All the tranquil and the still,
Like Sunday morning clear,
And mother's kitchen baking,
And kids at laughing play.

New Year

Squeeze out dark December,
Like toothpaste from the tube.
Roll up the end of this year
To push out uncertain remnants,
Before these hollow, leftover days,
Of famines, fears and follies,
Are wrung out, cast-off,
Thrown aside and no more.

In doing, know the trials, hurts,
Losses and disappointments,
Of this tiny touch of time,
Transform for those who trust
The power of a new calendar,
And the dropping of Time's ball,
To greater raise outlooks
For a changed and better life.

Stolen

Who stole my best mate away from me?
He's gone now an' I'm askin' you,
Who stole 'Arry McCaffety?
A mate ya could count on as true.

I remember, I remember the good times an' jokes,
Like when 'Arry and Billy and me,
Got into a scuff with some dry outback blokes,
Who'd come down to the coast from Taree.
Words were exchanged and no one was right,
An' it coulda turned into a brawl.
But 'Arry, he said, "It's too 'ot for a fight,
I'm gettin' beers from the pub for us all."

I spect ev'ry town has its one true light,
Its beacon shinin' through the dark.
One you can call on, any ol' night,
For a chat, or shoulder, or a lark.
One who is there when times are real rough,
When ya burd'ns are so 'ard ta carry,
An' ya wanna shout, "Enough is enough!"
For our town that true light was 'Arry.

I s'pose I should tell ya 'bout Lily,
Who came from the Smoke to teach in the school.
She was a beaut, who just happened to be:
A flower; a treasure; a jewel.
An' she was the one he could not do without.
An' she, it was plain, fell for 'Arry.
I saw it all and I had no doubt,
Lily's the girl he was goin' ta marry.

In winter he ask'd, and yes, she agreed.
They put out the word an' chose the day.
But Fate is a bitch. You'll pardon, I plead,
When I say it in such a coarse way.
She got real sick, then sicker, sicker still
'Til no sum of prayers, cries or tears,
Could rescue Lily from that terrible chill.
Now she'll ne'er see the turn of advancing years.

Who stole my best mate away from me?
Who stole 'Arry McCaffety?

'Arry threw it in. Joined up the army brigade.
Not so much for his country an' king,
But to still the pain 'er silence made,
And the rip of his heart—well, y'know the thing.
He weren't in for so very long, before
The army sent him far 'cross the sea,
And from our 'Arry, we 'eard—no more.
Gone now, lost in a place called Gallipoli.

Winters of Longing

Dreams that travel a lonely road
To a place that has no name,
Still meet the judgment
Of inner gods,
And the winters of longing in vain.

Hopes, so empty, so used,
Cannot change this time
That's now,
Nor make us see better
That which we really have.

Children Who Fell to Doom

Rising and falling, living and dying,
She knows silent sobs of lyke-wake crying.
For her mind holds children who fell to doom,
In cycles of her mortuary womb.
And the pounding in his chest, quick and deep,
Chases dreams; abruptly terminates sleep,
That in the cold night he wakes wet with sweat.
Two heavy hearts sadly paying nature's debt.
Two heavy hearts of longing and regret.

And the gap, the gulf, the distant growing,
Between two who vowed for life, but now knowing
What was solid, rock steady, had cracked.
The fault, ever spread by what their love lacked,
Grew wide, grimly threatening to destroy
For want of father's pride and mother's joy.
A childless life, for them, would not succeed,
Desire would not satisfy their need.
Desire would not awaken her seed.

Shivering

Shivering, shivering.
Winter's bite seemed early this year.
But the old woman could not be sure.
Time, for her, moved different now,
Since Frank's passing.

But she did know,
The terrible cold cut her bloodless fingers,
Turned laboured breath to melting ghosts,
And ceaseless chills stole snug sleep,
And neglected cracks seeped winded wet.

Yet, she wondered, was it cold enough,
Really, really cold enough,
For her to hobble next door,
And ask to borrow
Just a few small sticks of firewood?

Of Memories and Imaginings

Can one ever truly know
Just how they exist
In the mind of another?
One may ask,
They may tell,
Though the telling be filtered,
By assumed knowing,
Arrived at subconsciously,
Viewed through biased perceptions
Of memories and imaginings
Fashioned with incomplete awareness.

Can we truly know
How we exist
In the mind of another?

Greg Willson

Waiting Women

Here, where sparse, flat land gives way
To ever-changing green-grey sea,
And slow dancing waves lick gentle shore,
And lap, splash against mooring poles
Set deep and driven hard fast
At the other-world edge.
Here salt and sun-cracked men
Tie their little bobbing boats
And carry ashore their meagre catch
In baskets woven of reeds and care.

Here, empty now, is the common place
Where nets are dried and made good;
Tales widened by progressive tellings;
Catches compared; decisions made.
Where growing sons watch aging fathers,
And learn the talents of men of fish.

Here now group waiting women,
Of fish and sun and breathing sea,
With hands held to shade glare,
And shawl-covered heads,
And secret touches of unease in their breasts.
Watch, wait for sight of returning boats
As time turns and sun falls seaward.
And small children run at water's edge
And laugh in the red of closing day.

The waiting women strain and stretch their gaze
To shimmering line of sea and sky.
The little boats are late.
Returning time is come and passed,
And passed again some more.
Mood falls to a deeper place.
And playing children put aside their games
And draw in closer and fall quiet
As they clinging press to mother's legs.

Above, the shriek of hovering gulls,
Riding updrafts, floating, suspending gravity.
The gulls also wait and watch
For small sails of returning boats.

As unease turns to concern,
And strengths are measured in passing time,
The women's silent prayers are heard.
Just a speck of a wisp of sail,
Then straining twilight eyes see more,
Gradually growing closer, ever closer.
On shore, women mutely count
The distant, home-bound sails,
Until individual boats are recognised,
And in the last glimmer of sunlight,
Individual waving men are recognised.
Women, seeing men, return their greetings,
And cast aside the things they hide
Within their deep private selves.
And the shore is awash with unspoken relief.
And clinging children relax their hold and wave.
And yielding day gives way to folding night.

Greg Willson

Riding the Dog

Three days, three nights.
East coast to west coast.
Riding the Greyhound bus.
Ticket price has emptied my pockets.
Climb aboard, few seats left.
Sit next to an African American.
He's in army greens, on leave and chatty.
Talks of his home and girl.
Anxious to see both,
And the highway wheels keep turnin',
And the day keeps turnin'—into night.

Stop at a small diner, late into second day.
Get off. Stretch.
"Gettin' somethin' t' eat?" he asks.
"No, I'm on a diet," I say.
Only a partial lie.
He goes off. Ten minutes. Comes back.
Hands me a hotdog and soda.
Tells me, "Bin on a diet coupla times, myself."
We lean back against the side of the bus.
Silently watch Nebraska's setting sun,
And I eat the best hotdog I ever tasted.
Bus fills. We're moving west.
And the highway wheels keep turnin',
Keep turnin'. Keep turnin'.

Last Request

Death, where you hide and lurk I do not know,
But, certainly, you lie in wait for me.
I think of you as some cold, distant foe,
To be met, and there end my earthy spree.
Yet few may gaze upon that great knowing
With vision of where and when so clear,
As to count tomorrows they have owing,
And thereby judge you far or near.

Death, none do you exclude or overlook
As you gather each to your embrace.
No king, no queen, no bishop, knight or rook,
May escape your fatal end-game chase.
When you call and time is come and due,
And you cross my door, me to meet,
One last request would I ask of you:
Before you enter, kindly wipe your feet.

Bakehouse

Early in the morning,
The air is brittle as old twigs
And the grass on the ground
Is still cold with sleep.
The unbalanced sky has lost its dark,
Though not yet grown its light,
And whispers from unlit houses
Are wrapped in snores and quiet purrs.

And the only shriek of light,
And the only measured movement
In this Sunday-quiet, snoozing town,
Is within the little bakehouse
Already set at a humming pace,
Filling, thrilling the slumber-air
With a symphony of delicious smells,
Rising from the tested and the true.

And while the opening, yawning town,
Is still shaking off the night,
The bakehouse folds back its door.
Just a trickle at first; the early faithful.
But as morning shadows small,
The worn threshold busies
With the fleeting tread and travel
Of the townsfolk through the day.

Morning slips into afternoon.
The packed shelves thin; then sparse,
And the stir and steady pace eases.
Shadows stretch once more.
The sun dips and relaxes into night.
Town and townsfolk grow quiet.
At last, the bakehouse closes; sleeps.
Dreams of new breads, cakes and pastries.

Reach for Stars

Some will reach for stars tonight
Who lift questing eyes to see,
The spreading sweep and grandeur
Of a vast infinity.

And some will sense a smallness
Weighing Earth's geography.
Just a tiny blue dot, spinning,
Moving, turning constantly,
Around just another fiery star,
Towards an unknown destiny.

And some will gaze this stretching forth,
This open cosmic tapestry,
And view it through the lense of faith.
They, seeing only godly mystery,
Will turn it to a testament,
Of another invented theology.

And some, when asked what it's about
May speculate known reality,
As a simulated universe,
Computed holographically.
Created, coded by a future teen,
With too much time and acne.

Greg Willson

Yesterday and Tomorrow

While yesterday is growing still,
Tomorrow we have yet to fill.

Starting out with unsure step,
Can we know, or even guess,
The quickening, unfolding world,
Be it garden or grave,
We bestow or wreak upon
Our grandchildren's grandchildren?

Will they soar on wondrous wings
Of our caring construction,
Or trip, fall and fail,
Harvesting a terrible yield
From seeds sown this day and on;
Their hopes buried in the cold?

One hundred years and more,
When we are done and gone,
And our bed is but a box,
How will they, the yet unborn,
Peer through peeled back time
And measure our scorecard?

While yesterday is growing still,
Tomorrow we have yet to fill.

Just Dreaming

Last night I took a dreaming trip,
While soft the world was snoozing still,
And all who I had ever wronged,
Together stood, my dream to fill.

I saw the faces as they approached,
Unbidden though they surely be,
Of those I love and those called friend,
And even strangers they to me.

Each in turn came on this way
And there put voice to my dark sin,
While others stood to bar retreat,
Before I might, or dared, begin.

How bony fingers they did point,
And accusing eyes so coldly stared,
As babbled sounds from witches tongues
Shrilled ever high, my shame declared.

The line it stretched, oh, so far,
No just man ever right believed,
That such a one, damned as I,
Could of this world, be hell-conceived.

Now sun is stirring in the east,
And I smile as light is streaming.
My secret is still safe with me,
For I was, in sleep, just dreaming.

Wind, Sea and Ship

I am wind; savage, calm,
Howling and whispering;
Sweeping the foamy sea.
The dance and the dancer,
Moving the lifting wave,
Shaping the straining sail.
I push onward, ever onward,
From shore to distant shore.

I am sea; surface, deep,
Restless and changing;
Lifting, raging, vast.
Swelling, peak and trough,
On rushing and ebbing tide.
Inconstant as the wind,
I carry the ship; ocean and bay,
From shore to distant shore.

I am ship; mast and rig,
Sailing the shifting sea.
Bold hand to the wheel,
Sure eye to the course,
Correcting as I voyage on.
In storm and tranquil quiet,
I slice uncertain waters,
From shore to distant shore.

I am wind; I am sea; I am ship.

In 1962

Each Wednesday night was Ranch Night
At the local picture show.
And all the workday want-to-bes,
Hoppys, Genes and Roys,
Fronted favoured portal to flickering dreams
And lay their money down.

There was value in the darkness,
Newsreel, cartoon, cowboy double feature.
Goodies besting baddies
In rapt shoot-outs and big chase thrills.
Action adventures of sound and sight,
In those second-run, fantasies seen real.

And any brash back-row guy
Could be a hero to his best girl,
And keep her snug and safe and tight,
When danger threaten from the screen;
Or the theatre closed in tense and dark;
Or gripping fear choked the air.

All but vanished are those one-screen shows,
Now boarded up, or churches, furniture stores.
Moved along by multi-changing days.
But I fond remember the sweet, sweet times,
When Wednesday night was Ranch Night
Back in 1962.

South

The old man watched for a month or more.
Watched the vast, monotonous sky,
Watched for signs that did not show.
Just the ever-present sun, the endless glare,
Steadily baking him; the land; the sheep.
Steadily drying remaining water from the dam.

Rain had been thin and spare last year,
Now, essential, it appeared not at all.
The few fleeting clouds that did offer hope,
Drifted away below the horizon to the south.
He watched, waited, watched some more.
'Til time for watching and waiting passed.

It was just the old man and Jimmy now,
Since the boys had tossed in their share
For pursuit of bright city lights and life.
Just two men on horseback with three dogs,
Pushing sixteen hundred, scrappy sheep.
Get them south to feed and water, or lose the lot.

Six days out, beyond thirst, hunger, exhaustion.
The relentless sun assailing all.
The column stirred up dust, choked out air.
Here and there a sheep would stumble, fall.
They could not stop, they could not wait,
Could not chance the many for the few.

Mid-morning, the mob long strung out.
Near the top of a small steady rise
The lead animals stopped. Sniffed the air,
Sniffed, sniffed, and bolted up, over the crest.
Racing, tumbling, stumbling, pushing, crushing,
Down to the scant remnants of a once-lush dam.

Jimmy and the old man moved fast,
Wheeling the bulk of the frantic flock,
Turning them from unfolding bedlam below.
The dogs instinctively understood;
Raced to slow the advancing mob,
Nudging them out, away from smell of water.

With the greater number safely upwind,
The old man inspected the damage at the dam.
There lay the broken, crushed, drowned.
Those frantic to release the clutch of thirst.
But also a number calmly, quietly drinking;
Feeding on the sparse, edge grass.

Using the horses they cleared the carnage,
Up and over the opposite rise.
Then slowly, guardedly, little by little,
Guided the rest of the flock to drink.
There they stayed, rested, watered, fed,
All that day and through the next day, too.

He studied unchanging sky; kicked dust,
His hands pushed deep in empty pockets.
Could they chance to stay right here?
Could they hold 'til rain bonded life?
No. Too little feed, too little water.
The drought still held its threatening grip.

The old man did not count the losses.
Sheepmen survive on what they have,
Not on what has gone, or never was.
In the morning he mounted his horse,
Nodded at Jimmy; whistled to the dogs,
And they pushed the sheep further south.

Greg Willson

When We Are Gone

And trees will not mourn our passing,
Nor mountains or valleys regret.
Rivers and lakes will waste no tears.
Clouds will soft ride the pleasing breeze
Without a passing goodbye-thought.
Seas will continue to wash waiting shores.
Wind's tongue will not ask, will not tell,
And weather thick will ever form and fall.

And birds of the sky and fish of the sea,
Shall soar and swim as they did before.
Mammals, marsupials, reptiles and more,
Each in their own flight, foot and flow,
Will none proclaim, by shouts or whispers,
The vanishing of needless human clay.
And time tossing backward and forward,
Shall have a new telling of Earth's history.

All we have fashioned, created and made,
Will make no heartfelt plea for our return.
Pots, pans, cities, monuments and dams,
Will all crumble, rust, fail and decay.
Asphalt scars shall close over and heal,
And mornings and evenings will not pine,
As the natural world creeps, creeps,
Ever tip-toe creeps reclaiming its own.

In My Mind

In my mind I see it still
As a memory clearly new,
That little room atop the stairs,
Where we lived, and played, and grew.
The shadows on the window glass
Mottled through the giant tree,
I see it now as it was then.
I was six and you were three.

I still see the tire-swing
Turning slowly in the breeze,
The groan of rope on branch I hear
And your cry, "Faster, higher, please."
My mind yet holds the old bird-bath
We'd fill above the water line,
Then laughing splash the other for fun.
I was twelve and you were nine.

I'll not forget those special times
As we ran rivals for the ball,
Yes, I was older by three years
But you were game for all.
The street that night of noise and light,
And mother screaming on and on
And father holding her aside.
I was nineteen and you were—gone.

The Promise

"This I will promise you," he said,
"I know you know the lies I've fed,
I know I've really hurt you.
I'm done with it. I tell you true.
I know I've said I wouldn't, and I did,
Even knowing when I backward slid
My innocence I'd still proclaim.
I know my drinking's been to blame."

"You have my solemn word this time,
Though it may be an uphill climb,
I will do it! I tell you straight,
This promise I won't violate.
You can, from now, rely on me.
I'm through with drink, I guarantee,
No more will I ever cause you pain.
I'll never let you down again."

She smiled. Wiped her teary cheek,
Smiled at him, but did not speak.
She thought, I've heard it all before,
And edged away, quietly out the door.
He watched her go; watched door close.
What did her smile mean? Who knows!
He reached down the side of the chair,
And grasped the bottle hidden there.

Alone

But for the old man,
The house, like his world, is empty.
Long pressing silence;
Long heavy days;
Deep, dark, unending solitude.
Alone, alone.
Alone until he sleeps.

Then in dream they come to him,
Full, spirted, alive.
He is alone no more.
Family, friends, swell his world.
Smiling faces greet him,
His name upon their lips.
And there, the one he loved and lost,
Lifting his heart once more.

Morning drags him up from sleep,
And a blanket of loneliness
Swallows him;
Buries him in a deeper, darker place.
The house, like his world, is empty.
Another day, another day.

Gravity

There was a house when I was a kid.
It sat gently decaying under worldly weight,
A place to and of itself.
Silent and still, as the rest of the world went 'round,
Unwatching, uncaring, unmindfully turning
Ever more giddy about it.
A high, thick hedge hid it from show.
An unseen dog, barked at things beyond my knowing.
The only glimpse of the place was through double gates.
Metal, hard, cold and dark.
Misshapen, as if designed by someone gone insane.

Beware of the Dog warned the sign.
It rattled like a musical skeleton against the mad gates.
Did its job well.
I never saw anyone go through those gates.
Even hopeless salesmen walked by quickly, widely,
So its gravity wouldn't drag them in.
A lost sale preferable to a lost limb.

The garden was overgrown with weeds.
A few flowers, sickly-sad looking, struggled through.
They may as well have not bothered.

There lived in this house an old woman.
Stooped back, thin white hair, a walking shadow.
She seemed to have her own place,
One on, yet not truly of,
This vast, visible, twirling world.
Separate, pulling surrounds to the very core
Of her own secluded, removed and tiny universe.

Of Memories and Imaginings

I saw her a few times.
She would go to the mail box for letters that never came.
The other kids and I called her 'witch'.
We would hit the mad gates with sticks,
Then run off laughing.
If feeling especially brave we would chant:
"Witch. Witch. Witch..."
Then scatter, like dead leaves in a breeze,
If the curtains were pulled back.

I never knew her name; never cared to know.
In my day-to-day she was nothing to me.
Yet, I felt so empty inside, a sense of guilty grief,
The night I heard my father tell my mother,
"The old woman down the street was found dead today.
Said she'd died a week ago.
Might have laid there in that run-down house for months.
'Cept for that blasted dog howlin' all the time."

Christmas at Carrick Hill

A call went out and the Flower Ladies reply,
"Is it that time already? My how it does fly."
With the red, white and green, and with smiles and good cheer,
They roll up their sleeves and shortly get into gear.
And each to her task with her great love and fine skill,
They're decorating for Christmas at Carrick Hill.

The splendid tree, caringly dressed near the stairs,
Baubles, bows, a bright shimmering star it now wears.
And on the high roof it's not the widows who'll stray,
It's the man with the bag and the magical sleigh.
And when all is done, the sense, the sight, and the thrill,
They've decorated for Christmas at Carrick Hill.

Tribute Trees

Underfoot with each measured, solemn step,
Gravel crunches, crisp, short, sharp,
Along the military memorial walk.
Each side guarded by planted poplar trees.
Two long, thin, reverent rows
Standing tranquil, tall, true.
Silent sentinels in mourning mist.
Brass plates at the base of every tree,
Honouring each a single soul.
Those whose lives were lost,
Taken too soon to dark death.
Just a name joined by a rank,
From birth year, dash, to death year.
Entire lifetimes lived within dashes.
Compressed, compacted, concealed.
Everything each ever was or could be.
Everything, their total all,
Frozen forevermore in those brief dashes.
Gone now, taken in terrible times.
Gone now, almost fully forgotten,
Except for small, silent plates
At the base of tribute trees.

Greg Willson

Train Whispers

In the quiet of the time,
Comes the beckoning appeal,
Of the northbound, midnight train,
As it calls across the fields.
From the edge of the wooden porch,
When the moon hangs just so,
He can see the shadowy silhouette
Ghosting through the distant dark.

He thinks, as he's thought
A hundred, a thousand times before,
"One night I'll ride that train,
Forever gone from this dreary place.
Away to the city and a new life."
And in his imaginings he hears
The train whisper on the wind:
Youhavetogo youhavetogo youhavetogo.

By measured degree time moves on.
Each day an imperfect repeating
Of the day before, and before, before.
Each day the land takes back,
Until bit by scorning bit,
It's just he and his parents.
The harsh land has made them old,
And failed seasons taken all reserve.

And the work-weary parents
Know, without him there is no farm.
And he knows, without him,
The old folk cannot get by.
Now, out of his awakening,
Comes the sound from the tracks,
As the train whispers on the wind:
Youhavetostay youhavetostay youhavetostay.

The Plant, the Town, the People

The plant closed down eight months ago;
Took this sorry-coloured town with it,
And not one in three has drawn pay since.
Uncertainty threatens at one side,
Despair shadows the other,
As it tears towards a smalling future,
Of long, downward-looking faces,
And still longer welfare lines.

Here the wave and back-fence chatter,
Once the measure of shared days,
Is passed over, gone, defunct,
In this closed-in, closed-tight town.
Now familiars are with suspicion viewed,
As they sit remote, dispirited,
In their curtain-dimmed lives,
Lest others learn the little they have.

And for some sooner, some later,
Need displaces once-held pride.
And the charity-run foodbank,
They counted they would never need,
Now knows their hastened step
To be near the front of the line.
And from the gloomy grey of this year,
Next year, always next year, shines the hope.

I'm Coming Home

New leaves on a tree thought dead.
New thoughts in a once dull head.
I'm coming home, I'm coming home.
Could it be long winter's over?
Could it be spring's song's re-sung?
Or is this just a too-cruel dream
Condemning me to breathe another sun?

For winter's toll is taken,
And this body bows no more
To the dominion of the mind.
Now... now I long to tread that path
Where twisted trees straighten grow,
And withered branches charge with life,
And morning's shroud of mist is risen.

Let me leave skeleton twigs,
Pointing ashen fingers to the sky,
And soar beyond mortal reach,
Passed death's great stillness.
Through the tunnel to the light,
The way is patterned on my soul.
 I'm coming home.

Unfound Door

From familiar, folded shadows
Of their tight and tiny world,
They cautiously peer out,
See only that which threatens,
Or taps at false-held fears.

With neither plan nor purpose,
They withdraw, once more,
To their self-deceiving safety.
Then withdraw, once more,
To accustomed unawareness.

And the door is never opened,
For the door is never found.
The place to which it leads,
And all beyond, and on, and on,
Never seen, never known.

The unfound door
Remains hard closed,
And probably always will.
Its choices blind to view,
Though they be there yet still.

Those undiscovered choices,
Unseen, unsought, unexplored,
Those gateways to anew.
Waiting, evermore waiting,
Behind the unfound door.

Thomas and Emily

There is a tale long told from antiquity,
Of the ever-true love of Thomas and Emily.
Theirs was a love, far more than the word,
Beyond that ever known, ever seen, ever heard.
She was a beauty, both radiant and fair,
And his was the life she longed for to share.
Their bond was their all, so deep and so strong,
Gifting hopes and dreams, all their days long.

Now the lord of the land, jealous and cruel,
Eyed sweet Emily and lusted this jewel
To suffer first night with him in his bed,
Before giving herself to the one she would wed.
But Thomas and she of his scheme they did hear,
And planned to escape this lord and be clear
Of him, his rule and his right of first night.
Be gone before wrong could cut short their flight.

At the time agreed true hearts there did meet,
Dressed in their best, their plan now complete.
Each spotted, for purity, a ribbon of blue,
As they stood in the church and out of view
Of front door and guards of the lord of the land,
Sent for new wife once she'd given her hand.
But two, now one, knowing what was in store,
Stole away from the church through a side door.

Keeping church between they and the guard,
Man and wife ran earnest and hard,
To the pier with the little boat at wait,
To take two across wide waters straight.
They climbed aboard; the guards still blind,
They hoist the sail, their fate was signed.
The guards now saw and raced to the pier,
But boat and wedded lovers sailed out clear.

The lord of the land in his tower high
Saw all. Maddened his right they should deny,
Called upon wild spirits of wind and sea,
To rise up and force the boat back to the quay.
The sea did stormy rage, the wind frenzy roar,
Yet nothing could force fleeing boat back to shore;
Back to the guards; back to that wicked lord,
And back, back to his avenging sword.

Caught 'tween fatal sea and deathly shore,
Husband and wife together, ever, evermore.
As sea swallowed boat and wind wracked sail,
They clung to each other and there ended their tale.
Now below they do rest wrapped in eternity,
Together forever on that bed of the sea,
Together forever, united, stranded but free,
Stranded, stranded, stranded in the sea.

Walk With Me

Walk with me.
I, too, have been here before.
I, too, have known the dread and gripping darkness;
As captive in a self-set trap.
I, too, have felt the distance and cold isolation;
Closing in and closing out.
I, too, have seen the beckoning, smiling masks,
Hiding terrible, vicious teeth.
Yet though the way seems frightful now,
Walk with me.
I, too, have been here before,
And I know the way out.

A Memory Lost

Where goes a memory lost?
Is it lost forever,
Like a shadow shaped at night,
Caught up in a stir of entangled time,
Fragmented, torn and pulled apart,
Dead, buried and greedily devoured
By troops of eager guttle worms,
Until, as if, it never was at all?
A between-the-ears index card washed clean.

Or does it still somewhere linger,
Whole, part, shrivelled up,
Alone, paired or a-swarm,
Lying just beyond wakeful reach,
Holding on by cerebral fingertips,
Timidly peering out from grey, wet stacks,
Within the library of the mind?
Taking care, everywhere, not to be seen.

Or does it softly, quietly drift,
Detached from its once-moorings,
A floating, aimless, gliding wanderer,
In the river of abandoned yestertime,
Silently nodding, mind-bobbing by,
Waiting to be fished out, splutter splash,
Recognised, remembered, rescued,
And returned to the waiting, wondering fold?
Where goes a memory lost?

The Rising

Beneath the living, breathing skin,
A thousand generations
Of daisy-chain heartbeats,
Father, mother, father, mother,
Absent from this lifetime,
Now stir, mix and merge,
In a gathering unknown, unseen.

There blends a new awakening,
As it steadfastly expands,
And bubbles to the crowding top,
Of the ever-gifting pool.

And each in his stillness,
And each in her silence,
Though backwardly diminishing,
Adds by pound or by pinch,
Their own portion to the rising.

Flying Kites on Sunday

Feel the run and the rush
And the tug of the climb,
As the wind sweeps under,
Driving it up first time.

Just an old stocking tail,
Two sticks and some string,
Glue, paper and cloth,
It's now the *Sky King*.

Every eye fixed upward,
Willing it rise higher,
While line is played out
By the earth-bound flyer.

And I stand and I watch
From a distance, you see,
Outsider to this band
Of kiters flying free.

I remember when I,
More years than can say,
Would strain at the line
Flying kites on Sunday.

Birthday Lottery

Going Out

They're marching in the street today.
You can hear the Army band,
And the measured step, step, step,
Of the troop of passing greens,
Slouch hats and polished boots.
Young faces, new from basic training.
On each side the excited swarm,
With cheers and little waving flags.

Politically pressed suits and ties
Make speeches of freedom, honour,
While brass-button coats
Drum and fife them across the sea.
Away to fight another war,
In a place they do not know.
And faces of the farewell crowd,
Show pride, yet strange unease.

South Vietnam

Twelve days aboard the *Sydney*,
Then Chinook to Nui Dat.
Just a name, no understanding yet,
Of the pain; the sacrifice ahead.
Each day a fresh-baked hell.
The constant, strangling heat,
And the rain. God, the rain!
As if sheer terrors were not enough.

On patrol. Dense shadow jungle,
Paddy fields of clinging mud.
Fighting can change boys to men,
Turn men to greater, or lesser, men.
Booby traps, snipers, landmines,
Tunnels, wounded, body count.
Search and destroy. Kill or be killed.
And a stench that won't wash off.

Home

A year gone, back aboard the *Sydney*,
Returning to Australia.
Not the homecoming of earlier troops,
No parade, no *Waltzing Matilda*.
Now open scorn. Anti-war movement.
Protest signs: *Murderer*; *Scum*.
No debriefing; no deprogramming,
Just tour's up, now fend for yourself.

Time moves, fighting ceases.
Gone now the signs; disgusted looks.
Fewer the unanswerable questions,
'So, what was the war like?'
But still delayed stress reactions:
Depression; sleeplessness; nightmares.
The horror they left, will not leave them.
Maybe it never will.

Country of Myself

Wherever I rest my sight,
I see myself there reflected back.
I am both the one looking out,
And likewise, the one looking in.
Seeking an abstract reality,
In this, the country of myself.
I am, as a curious stranger,
At once both found and lost.

And from beginning to present,
Whether in famine or abundance,
Alone or in company shared,
I know I have come a far piece,
Exploring this inner territory,
And all I choose to consider.
I colour the space of my days,
And transfer think to ink.

Rotary Kids

Clothes on the line
Looked more like kids
Going 'round on a carnival ride.
Red kids,
Green kids,
Blue kids,
Spotted kids,
Chequered kids,
Shirt kids,
Towel kids,
Underwear kids.

Kids of all shapes and sizes
Who paid twenty-five cents
To be pegged up
By their thumbs
For the ride.

Greg Willson

The Port and the Container Terminal

The port was the very centre of the universe.
Ships arrived daily under colours of many nations.
Glad-to-be-ashore drunken seamen
Reeled, fought, swaggered, spat and stumbled
In narrow, cobblestone lanes,
While scarlet girls jangled cheap jewellery
And competed for the mean and pressing trade.

Ships sliced through shimmering silver water,
And bright banners bridged bustling streets.
Tradesmen whistled at their work;
Sailors sang songs of faraway lands
And seabirds joined in shrieking chorus;
While on the wharves, amid shouts and clatter,
Big men with faded singlets, tattoos,
Hair on their backs, obscenities on their lips,
Toiled and strained in the yellow heat of day
And under the white flare of lights at night.
And the smell of salt, from sea and sweat,
Was raw in the air.

But all that was before the opening
Of the container terminal further up the coast.
Before the rude terror of technology;
Before proud men withered into lost children;
Before futures came with question marks,
And boredom became the substance filling days.

Of Memories and Imaginings

Gone now the ships, and the hustle, and the noise.
Gone now the seamen, the songs, and the girls.
Gone now the shipping agents, the tally clerks,
The businesses that once worked eagerly
Satisfying the varied demands of the port.
Replaced by echoes in empty warehouses,
Brick-shattered windows, unemployment,
Dispirited old men, deserted workplaces,
Boarded up shop fronts, crude graffiti,
And the shiver of silent shadows at night.

Clamour and glamour became despair;
Colour ran to disease-grey, and the wharves,
Once alive, now held vessels at rest and at rust.
Decay descended over the streets, the buildings,
The down-turned faces of uncertain people
Stranded in this soul-stripped place.
And the smell of salt, from sea and tears,
Was raw in the air.

Moonta 1873

The little ones are sleeping tight,
Wrapped snug in cemetery grounds.
And all that they have left to show
Are haunting little mounds.

Tread softly as you pass them by,
These places they now stay.
These tiny, nameless unmarked graves,
Of children taken from their play.

Three crept into this copper town
When it was young and raw,
Three called children to their rest,
Two, three hundred, a hundred more.

Both diphtheria and cholera
Each took a modest share.
But it was fever typhoid,
That caused most of the despair.

The littles, they sleep tonight,
Their beds of earthy brown,
Unnamed, yet remembered still,
In quiet Moonta town.

The Arrival

She came with the wild, wet winds of winter,
As day eased aside the night,
And mist cradled a clinging chill,
Muffling each thin murmuration.
Her eyes, players of life unspoken,
Truth-tellers of her inner tale.
As the morning, they lay quiet, dark, deep,
Like sometime strangers to colour and light.

She was cold, wet and windblown,
Seemingly lost. Lost and hungry.
Yes, I'd seen that look before.
A memory from the pain part of my mind.
I said nothing, just opened wide the door.
An invitation. She hesitated; held back,
Then entered, needing to trust someone,
Needing to belong somewhere.

She accepted the offered meal,
And with unsure eyes asked more.
Day passed. Distance narrowed.
Clearly she did not desire to depart.
Beyond doubt, I did not want her to go.
And that night, as cold again came creeping,
Together we took to keeping each other warm.
Cats really can make themselves at home.

Greg Willson

Today

Today. Today I shall ride the train
To the very end of the line.
Far beyond the place I always alight,
Far beyond the habitual, understood and safe.
I shall let the known, the everyday,
The well-worn, trite and commonplace,
Just whiz by as I stay aboard,
Bound for where I have never been.

Today. Today when my journey is done
And I, in discovery, alight the train
Where others of my station never step.
I shall open my eyes to a realm unseen,
Listen to the hum of hurry not heard,
Smell, touch and taste a newfound world
As I rise above the common man,
A new Magellan; a new Armstrong.

Today. Today I will walk unfamiliar streets,
Bound the steps of life three at a time,
Embrace the foreign, the new.
A changed, more conscious and better me,
One who seeks out fresh excitements,
And new-made, treads the uncommon path.
Leaving others to the this and thating
Of their secondary, vicarious lives.

Today. Today I will stamp myself anew.
Today the world loses a ticky-tacky, boxed-in,
Programmed, button-downed, umbrella man,
And gains one who boldly strides out,
One who defies the pattern and the line.
One who turns a... Oh, I almost forgot,
There's a movie I want to see,
I better leave the train where I always do.

On Gazing at a Photograph of Myself as a Child

If I could have known you then,
With all that I know now.
If I could have whispered secret in your ear,
A warning of blind, fumbling pitfalls ahead,
Blown in on the surging, rustling winds of time.
If I could have spoken clear with you then,
And laid for you a map of coming days,
Showing discovered roads to take and avoid
In your maze-wanderings through life.
Would I have done so?

Actions change history.
Just one seemingly insignificant thing:
A road untaken; a stone unturned,
May warp an uncertain, trembling future,
May collapse new lines of dominoes ,
To tumble to better or worse,
And mint a new reality into being.
Altered, unseen waves
Stretch and form new crests, new troughs,
As one change sets off a hundred more.
Would I have chanced it?

One Perfect Tree

He came to these woods just a short year ago
With axe and rope and warm Christmas glow.
He wanted to find that one perfect tree
To take home for Billy and Molly and he.
Now again, in truck, with carols singing,
And world with loved ones, doorbell-ringing,
And bright, happy faces alive with joy,
Every man and woman, girl and boy.

He returned to select one perfect tree.
Different, this year, as it needed to be.
Larger, of course, last year's was too small.
A lot can change in a year and all.
He'd gone deeper into the woods this time,
To lessen discovery of the crime.
A lot can change in a year, it's true,
To all, everyone, to me and to you.

Then chance looking up, there happened to be
The goal he had sought, that one perfect tree.
Perfect. As if Heaven and Earth did collide.
And there he hanged himself in suicide.

M.V. Blythe Star

October weather moves and seesaws,
Catching incoming tide, swelling waves,
Whipping white foam to land,
Spiriting clouds of salty spray
To mist the cold morn rising.
In such moments, more rare now,
I can look along the melting shore
And almost see that rock-drenched coast
Of cliffs, sheer, rough and cruel.
Almost hear the fearful silence,
Split only by a wall of wind, gulls,
And crashing sea against steadfast rock.

In vision I see them staggering, stumbling,
From life raft to stony shore.
Faces stricken, stretched beyond weak;
Survival food gone, water gone.
Each blundering close to beckoning death,
One already wrapped snug in the deep.
Nine falling to savage land; to the place
Where two more crewmates
Will lay to breathe their last.
While capsized, sunken beneath the waves,
Ten terrible drifting days away,
Rests the motor vessel, Blythe Star.

Greg Willson

A Father's Sons

The twins were almost four
When she finally left him.
Took the two boys.
Moved back home to her parents.
Finally found courage and left.
Left the foul language; the abuse.
Left the unbroken stench of drunkenness.
Left the ever-threatened violence.
She waited so long.
Too long, others said,
She hoped sons might transform him,
Might awaken an inner swell of fatherhood,
Might forge them into a real family.
But nothing changed—or would,
No matter how she hungered it.

And time passed and they grew.
He never saw them—or wanted to.
They never saw him—or wanted to.
It was somehow ironic; karmic,
That when Brian and Colin were twelve
Their father was hit and killed
By a drunk driver.

They grew some more, and more,
'Til at twenty they moved.
Away from their mother,
Away from their grandparents,
Away from each other.
Each into lives of their own creating,
Each further distanced from the other
Until dispossessed of contact.

Of Memories and Imaginings

In their widening separateness
Brian and Colin chose opposing roads.
Colin went from one nothing job
To the next nothing job,
As he moved around
Barely ahead of his festering debts.
He drank evermore frequently
'Til drinking replaced everything else.
All his meaning and substance of life
Swilled at the bottom of a bottle.
And asked how he came to be
The man he had become,
Colin replied:
"With my father as role model,
What would you expect?"

Brian grew into a good job,
Applied himself, gradually moved up.
Married, bought a nice house,
Had children, laughed often,
Built, guided and loved his now family.
And asked how he came to be
The man he had become,
Brian replied:
"With my father as role model,
What would you expect?"

Greg Willson

The Distance of Things

He loved to pace the distance of things.
It enlivened, energised, electrified
And stirred something primal, sexual,
In the circuitry of his uncharted mind.
Along. Left, right, left.
Across. One, two, three.
Around. Etcetera, etcetera.
On and on, feet pounding,
Legs striding, head counting,
Excitement building.

He knew it all:
The number of steps
Between his mother's house
And the bicycle shop;
Where the half-way point was;
The quarter, the three-quarter.
How many steps across the park;
Over the bridge; through the tunnel;
Between the church and the post office;
The police station and the school.

All recorded in a square, tattered,
Side-spiral notebook.
Page upon page of small-scrawl numbers.
He would open the much-used book,
Look at the numbers and smile,
Recalling their where and when.
Somehow, to him, it seemed important;
Seemed to still commonplace fears;
Shine light on dark haunts
And make the world less brutish.

If I Could

If I could take a page writ now,
And read it fifty years ago,
Would the reading me be changed somehow,
Could I know then what I did not know?

If I could see the future me,
And look on now through younger eyes,
Would that vision invite prosperity,
Could I perceive the truth from lies?

If I could know ahead in time,
And understand its inference,
Would there be reason or rhyme,
Could that knowing make a difference?

If I could start again once more,
And be aware of each new sowing,
Would I do as I did before,
Could I be better for the knowing?

Greg Willson

Morning Soliloquy

Good morning, Beautiful Lady.
I've always loved this photo of you.
Then, I guess my bias is cut in your favour.
See, I'm wearing the suit you helped me pick.
The one for our fiftieth wedding anniversary.
Fifty years, a long time some may say.
But, for me, it passed so quickly—too quickly.
Right now, I'd give anything,
For just one more day with you.

Jennifer is bringing her car to pick me up.
She said, Doug will take the two boys.
She's a good girl, our Jen.
Phoned four times yesterday.
Just to make sure I was alright.
Even offered to stay over last night, if I wanted.
I told her I could sleep in this house by myself.
After all, I did it all the time you were in hospital.
She worries this will be too much for me.

They took me to see the funeral place.
Beautiful, and real nice people.
Showed me where the coffin will be.
I'll be sitting just three or four arm lengths from you.
Others will probably be watching me.
See how I'm holding up.
They mean well, I know they do.
But I'm not sure I can bear one more person
Telling me how very, very sorry they are.

I Could Have Been a Sailor

I could have been a sailor,
There are worse things to be sure.
I could have lived my life
Bobbing Neptune's green-grey way.
With a ship as my home,
And the world as my address;
Schooled in the steady rise and fall
Of the nervous, nomadic flow.

I could have been a sailor,
Come to read the ways of sea.
Known sextant, compass and chart;
Set practiced hands upon the helm;
Learnt to drink; learnt to swear,
And knot and splice a rope.
Lived the life a seaman gains,
And the life he gives away.

I could have been a sailor,
Could have felt the pitch and push
Of the boiling, foaming sea.
And tasted the salt of angry spray,
And gazed at night's abounding stars,
Sharp and clear and white,
And measured my small, small place,
In the endless universe.

I could have been a sailor,
Lived a fugitive from the shore.
Shared life and labours and laughs,
With brothers of the brine.
But I'm glad I'm not a sailor,
Though tempting that may be,
For if I were a sailor,
I may never have known you.

Rose and Son

It was a bleak, disagreeable looking building,
Much like the unordered, bleak looking workforce,
Sharing shallow griefs and uninspired pace,
Drawn to this edifice of dulled despair.
It stood unprotected in separateness,
Ostracised by its architectural fellows.
Alleyways each side; back forsaken.
Moated, marooned both outside and in.

Rose and Son, Makers of Finest Boutique Paint
Announced the tired sign at the company face.
Rose senior wilted, withered and died,
Leaving 'Son' to mismanage the business.
Mover, shaker, paint pumping through his veins,
Elder Rose was passionate, decisive and resolute.
This, 'Son' never was. No feeling; no desire.
Younger Rose simply failed to rise.

The office was atop plain, narrow stairs,
Hollowed by years of reluctant feet.
An uninviting door, needing work,
And grimy, light-rejecting windows,
Ensured only the most mentally misshapen,
The easy misled or hawker unbidden,
Could mistake heart-shrinking reality.
But enough were so blind to busy the door.

He Who Never Tries

I heard a voice say unto me
That it was all too hard,
That this and that and something else
Was hurting life's scorecard.

And someone else agreed with it,
Another said the same.
It seems that almost everyone
Is 'bout to quit the game.

But those who see success and gain
In Victory's bright eyes,
Know the only one who truly fails
Is he who never tries.

One House

Part One

He sat in his car, three houses down.
Saw the large removalist's van pull up,
Backwardly advance onto the driveway.
A car stopped outside the house.
Family of four burst out. New occupants.
He sat, watched excited animation,
Watched other belongings moving in,
And new owners take down the 'sold' sign.

He remembered when he and his new bride
Moved their possessions into that house,
The garden they planted, they tended.
The home where they also became four.
One bad decision; all doomed to the bank.
'For sale' sign up and downed wife in tears,
Their children looking lost and asking:
"But what about our friends?"

Part Two

The old house stands empty now,
And gone are the glad-held days,
When house eclipsed its summed parts,
And living brimmed within this space,
And the warming sounds of family,
Friends, neighbours, pets and more,
In spirited comings and busy goings,
Thrilled, filled these rooms now still.

Closed up, locked up, lifeless,
Another 'sold' sign in the front yard.
Vacant, except for sepia memories
There lingering, haunting, hovering still.
Silently it waits for the moving rumble,
And the coarse, savage assault
Of developer's bulldozer and heavy trucks.
Clear the old for the future new.

Journey

What true eye can trace a track
Through close and stony course,
Where heat of day and chill of night
Mark sure the journey steep?

And what strong heart can ease the load
As it increases day and dark,
When a barren, desolate mind,
Is fixed to a former way?

A rough, dark valley lies ahead,
Bleak and dim as those before.
A further weary reaping of
The random seeds once sown.

On that rock-filled valley floor
A vision bold to charge the blood,
Standing, clearly, quietly beckoning,
One last chance in a hard, hard world.

Heart renewed rallies leaden feet
To tread light the path between;
And unleashed mind with wings does fly,
From treason's last redoubt.

Forward the step, onward the trek,
Released from the self-made yoke.
While heart and feet, together beat,
A quickening of pulse and purpose.

The Writing and the Wronging

Today is yesterday and yesterday's tomorrow,
And I can't think of time in a straight line no more.
The lady over there carries bags she had to borrow
When the keeper of good people shut her out the door.

Life is moving much too fast, pushing pictures of the past
Against a crazy now we're trying to ignore.
There's the hurry, there's the slow pace,
There's the hidden, there's the show place,
There's the writing and the wronging on the wall.

And the judging eyes and pity, follow us about the city,
Where's the reason, where's the justice to it all.
They all decide, they all determine
Who's the cream, who's the vermin,
Who's the upper, who's the lower on the stack.

And for us there'll be no entry in that book of five-star
    gentry,
No big farewell when the slab is at our back.
We're the homeless, we're the nameless,
We're the guilty, we're the blameless,
We're the writing and the wronging on the wall.

Once and Now

Once stood a stallion,
Spirited, proud and strong,
Impatient for unloosing
To the forceful quest:
Where time flew on hoof
In haste to the finish;
Where ride and rider
Lay fallen, spent as one.

Now snorts its uneasy ghost,
With just thin memories
Of charging to that end.
Passed long shadows
Of shielded cannon,
That howled in heat
In times before,
In times... times before.

And for just a moment,
A head may faintly lift
And look dolefully back,
Along that narrowing road.
Look back... look back
From now to then,
And see the dimming past,
Spent and fallen.

The Wondrous Purple Box

The gods of plenty reached out.
Reached out and touched us,
And the purple box we found.
It was not a big box.
At least, not as I remember it.
But inside, within its box-walls,
Oh, my... Inside it held
The makings of a child's world.

My sister saw it first.
She said, 'Finders keepers.'
But I was eight and she was five,
So, naturally, we shared.
It contained everything needed
For a wondrous childhood.
Even a full, life-size circus,
With elephants and everything.

Greg Willson

House on Mercer Street

It's quite a small house,
For such a giant of a man.
That house at one, one, two.
I started out at dawn.
Edison to Princeton.
Could have taken the train,
But it's only forty minutes by car,
Back to mid-twentieth century.

I park one block over
And walk to Mercer Street.
I want to get a sense of the place
And feel the morning sun.
It's still, save for breeze on leaves,
It's quiet, save for lone passing car,
And the sound of my own footfall
Following along the sidewalk.

I stand on the opposite side of the street,
Hands thrust deep in pockets.
Savour the growing warmth, and the house.
Then cross over; walk where he walked,
In this peaceful place set apart
From the clatter of eternal change;
Sheltered by these white wooden walls,
In this, his home for twenty years.

As morning opens gently by,
It's just me, the house and the tiptoeing sun.
No words can improve the silence.
I smile at everything and nothing,
Breathing a tiny slice of his world.
Profound happiness is my only reality
Standing out front of Einstein's home.
Dancing, anyone?

I Am the Dreamer

What I now reveal will shock to extreme,
For you and your world are really my dream.
The book in your hand, the thoughts in your head,
I dream them all, mark well what is said—
    I am the dreamer!

All you perceive on such a vast scale,
I make it all to the smallest detail.
From me flow the memories creating your past,
I dream them all, from the first to the last—
    I am the dreamer!

All you taste, touch, hear, smell and see,
Is not from your senses, it's from me!
You laugh at my words and think I'm insane,
Can you guess who put that thought in your brain?
    I am the dreamer!

There's no escape, no place to hide,
From the dream I dream with you inside.
When morning's first light streaks the sky,
I will wake, and you will die—
    I am the dreamer!

Time-Out

Through the comings and the goings,
Of overhasty times,
I've known the trickle and the flood.
From steady drip, drop, dripping,
To full and fevered spill.
As emotions, quickened and unstuck,
Construct their own bull-headed reality,
And preach unbound expansion.

Both the black and the white,
Each adding to, then lost to,
A swirling, mingling grey.
Each taking each to the edge of overflow
In mounting rally upon rally,
Serve attack, return defence.
Blinkered, passed rocky outer-reaches
Of better judgment; better reason.

And if, at times as these:
Times of one pointing out,
Blind to three pointing back,
I had froze the moment;
Paused the ever-pressing force;
Allowed calm to take the field.
Time-out may have been the sane choice.
Time-out may have made all the difference.

Lady of the Night

Standing by an open door,
I watch the golden lantern,
Follow a path
In memory of
Florence Nightingale,
Treading silent darkness
Between wounded days,
In times now past.

Lady of the night,
The pain of loneliness
Shows upon your face,
As you sail ever on.

Once, I paused and watched
An eagle,
Proud and strong,
Swoop at your tranquillity,
And I remember that victory cry
As you lost your innocence
In one small step,
In one giant leap.

Lady of the night,
The pain of loneliness
Shows upon your face,
As you sail ever on.

And beliefs, on reflection,
To you drawing, directing;
Mind, tide, weather and more,
In myth or fable, fact or fancy,
Will surely wane,
As you slowly, ever so slowly,
Fingernail away,
Lady of the night.

Greg Willson

Sleepy Warm

The worst form of violence is surely that which is inflicted against us by those we look to for our very protection.

T. P. Carolat

Part One

Dad ain't home yet.
Like most nights.
I hears Mum movin' 'bout the place.
She comes in and tells me to get up.
I's got me jammies on.
She sez to put on me dressin' gown.
I likes me dressin' gown.
It's warmer than jes' me jammies.
If I had slippers I'd put them on.
But I don't.
Mum gets Denny up.
She wraps a blanket 'round him.
Denny don't got no dressin' gown.
Mum's bin cryin'.
The cut on her mouth must be hurtin'.
Mum tells me to get Teddy.
Teddy is mine.
I lets Denny hold him sometimes.
But Teddy's still mine.
Mum carries Denny and holds me hand.
I hold Teddy.
We goes out the front.
There's a taxi car out there.
Mum opens the back door and puts Denny in.
Mum tells me to get in, too.
I push passed Denny.
I wants to be next to the winder.
Mum puts in two shoppin' bags with our clothes in.
Mum gets in next to Denny.
She tells the taxi car man somethin' I don't hear.
I's never bin in a taxi car before.

I look out the winder with Teddy.
Mum wipes her eyes.
The taxi car drives off.
I wanna wind down the winder.
Mum sez, No.
We drive some more.
Mum don't say nothin'.
We stop at a big buildin'.
Mum sez for me to get out.
She carries Denny.
Mum tells me to carry the bags with clothes.
They are big an' I'm only five.
Mum sez I'm a big boy now.
She wipes her nose.
I puts Teddy under me arm.
Mum gives some money to the taxi car man.
She counts in out real slow.
The taxi car man drives away.
We stand in the street not sayin' nothin'.
Me feets is cold.
I don't got no shoes on.
Mum holds Denny an' takes one o' the bags.
I hold Teddy proper now.
We go in the buildin'.
I asks, What place is this?
Mum sez, It's somewhere safe.

Part Two

I's playin' cars with Curtis.
We don't got no cars.
We jes' move our fingers on the floor an' make car noises.
Curtis come to the shelta day 'fore yestd'y.
His Mum brung him with her.
Curtis is me best friend now.
He sez his Mum had a bad sperience with he's Dad.
I don't know what sperience means.
But I nods anyways.
Curtis is five, same like me.
Mum comes down the hall.
Mum sez Dad telephoned up the shelta.
She sez she talked to him.
Mum is like she's happy now.
Ya can hardly see the cut on her mouth no more.
Mum sez, Dad is real sorry.
She sez, He wants us to come back home.
Curtis stops playin' preten' cars.
He listens to Mum, too.
Mum sez, Dad will pick us up out the front.
She sez for me to come.
Say goodbye to your friend, she sez.
I sez, Goodbye.
Curtis looks sad.
Mum an' me goes down the hall.
I looks 'round at Curtis.
He jes' sits on the floor.

We waits for Dad outside.
Mum holds Denny.
The bags with our clothes is next to us.
I holds Teddy.
We waits.
Mum sez, It'll be different this time.
Dad has changed.
Denny cries a little bit.
Mum pats he's back.

Dad arrives in he's ute.
He leans over an' opens the passenga door.
He sez, Get in.
Mum puts the bags in back o' the ute.
We gets in.
Mum holds Denny.
I squash's in the middle with Teddy.
Dad leans and kisses Mum.
Me an' Teddy gets more squashed.
Mum is like she's happy.
We drives off.
Dad sez we all back togetha now.
Dad is smilin'.

We gets home.
Dad smiles to Mum.
Mum smiles back.
Dad sez, I was nice this time,
I won't be so nice if there's a next time.
Mum stops smilin'.

Part Three

I's talkin' quiet with Teddy.
We gotta be real quiet coz Dad's sort o' sleeping in he's chair.
I's whispas close to Teddy's ear.
Then I puts Teddy close to my ear.
Teddy whispas back likes he tells a secret.
Teddy sleeped in Denny's cot last night coz Denny was cryin'.
Dad's like he's angry when Denny cries.
Teddy's back with me nows.

Mum comes in.
She sez to Dad, Kingsley's at the front door.
He sez you owe him for a bet.
Dad looks at her with he's not happy face.
Kingsley lives next door.
Dad don't like Kingsley.
Kingsley works in a office.
Dad sez people what works in a office is bludgers.
Dad gets outa he's chair an' sez a not-nice word.
He looks like he's angry.
He sez, Give me a dolla from the housekeepin'.
Mum looks like she's upset, but don't say nothin'.
She gets her purse an' hands Dad a dolla coin.
Dad goes into the kitchin.
Mum follas 'im.
She sez, Now I'm gonna be short this week.
I takes Teddy.
We stills bein' real quiet.
We stands by the kitchin door.
Dad gets pliers from the drawer.

He lights the gas burna with a match.
Dad holds the dolla in the fire with the pliers.
Mum sez, What are ya doin'?
Dad stares at her like he's lots angry nows.
He sez, Shut it, woman.
Mum stops talkin'.
The dolla gets sort o' red.

Dad puts it on a plate.
He takes the plate with the dolla down the hall.
Dad opens the front door.
Teddy an' me's move to the hall an' watches.
Kingsley is outside.
Dad holds out the plate like it's a special present.
Never say I don't pay up, sez Dad.
He tips the plate so the dolla starts t' slide off.
Kingley puts he's hand unda t' catch it.
The dolla falls off the plate.
Kingley catches it in he's hands.
Kingsley makes a cry out noise.
He drops the dolla.
Dad laughs an' shuts the door.
He sez t' Mum, That'll teach the poofta.
Dad sees me an' Teddy watchin'.
He sez, Boy, learn from the masta.

Part Four

Mum sez I's getting' some shoes t'day.
We goes to the church shop where we gets our clothes.
They got no shoes my size.
We gets on a bus an' drives to the big shops.
I likes the bus.
I turns on the seat and looks at the peoples.
A lady smiles at me.
Mum holds Denny.
We gets to the big shops.
I waves goodbye to the lady.
Mum makes me try on lots of shoes.
Denny sits on the floor.
Mum keeps pushin' the outsides of all the shoes.
I asks Mum why.
She says she needs to check for toe-room.
I don't understand, but she smiles.
Toe-room must be a good thing.
After a long time Mum sez, This pair.
I sez, Can I wears them home?
Mum sez, No.

Dad coms home.
He looks like he's angry.
I's takes Teddy and we tries to keep outa the way.
Dad sits at the table.
Mum puts down a plate with toast an' bake beans.
Dad looks at the plate then looks at Mum.
Mum sez, Sorry, that's all there is.
Dad looks mean angry.
He sez loud, A man works all day an' all he gets is this.
Mum sez she's short this week.
Mum sez she had to buy me shoes.

Dad looks at me with he's angry face.
I holds Teddy real close.
Mum sez, He starts school next week.
Dad don't say nothin'.

He picks up the plate and throws it at the wall.
The plate breaks.
The toast and bake beans make a mess.
Dad stands up an' knocks he's chair over.
Teddy and me moves away.
Mum starts to say somethin'.
Dad grabs her hair.
He sort of swings her an' she hits the wall.
Dad looks at me an' Teddy.
He says, Come here.
Mum slides down on the floor.
Teddy an' me's a bit scared.
Dad sez, I said, come here.
Dad looks lots angry now.
I moves a bit to Dad.
Mum sez, Don't hurt him.
Dad don't look at Mum.
I looks at Mum an' Dad grabs me.
He pushes me back into the wall.
I falls over.
Me back hurts from crashing in the wall.
I's holdin' Teddy so's he's safe.
Dad turns an' pushes another chair over.
He walks loud to the front door an' goes out.
He bangs the door shut.
Mum's cryin' and reaches an' holds me.
We's sittin' on the floor.
Teddy looks sad.

Part Five

Dad come home late 'gen t'night.
He's cross at somethin'.
Mum don't get cross back.
'Stead she gets Dad some beer an' sez, Watch some TV.
Dad sits an' goes t' sleep.
Dad sleeps in he's chair lots o' nights.
We's always got to be's quiet.

Mum sez for me's to put on me dressin' gown.
She sez, Get Teddy.
Mum gets Denny an' sez, Be real quiet.
We goes out the back door.
Mum sez, Come on.
She's got Dad's keys an' opens the ute door.
Again she sez, Be real quiet.
I gets in with Teddy.
Mum puts Denny in the middle.
She puts some stuff in the back.
Mum gets in the driver's side.
She starts the car and drives out.
I looks at Mum but don't say nothin'.
Dad don't let Mum drive he's ute.
He's gonna be real angry.
Dad sez, Women shouldn't be loud t' drive.
Denny an' Teddy an' me's sit still.
I asks, Where we goin'?
Mum sez, Where he can't hurt us ever again.
We stops at a place where they's no houses.
It's dark an' sort o' like a track.
Mum sez, Stay in the car.
She gets out an' takes things outa the back.
I hears her doin' stuff but don't know what.

After a little bit she opens the passenga door.
I's start to gets out but Mum sez, Stay.
I holds Teddy an' Denny's still in the middle.
Mum winds the winda down a bit.
She puts in the end of a hose and winds the winda up again.
I looks at her.
She puts in a towel at the top of the winda.
I asks, What's that for?
Mum sez, To keep us cozy.
She shuts the passenga door.
Mum comes 'round the front an' gets in the driver's side.
She has a box with cakes.
She gives one to me an' one t' Denny.
She starts up the ute, but we don't go nowhere.
We jus' sits and eats an' warm comes outa the hose.
Mum takes a envelope outa her bag.
I asks, What letta is that?
Mum sez, It tells our story.
She sez, I love you both.
Mum's got cry tears on her face.
I sez, I love you too, Mum.
The warm from the hose gives me a little headache.
I don't sez nothin'.
I's a big boy now.
The cakes is yummy.
I sorta gettin' sleepy.
I smiles at Mum an' Teddy.
Denny sorta smiles.
Denny looks sleepy, too.
We's all quiet.
Jus' the noise o' the mota comin' through the hose.
An' sleepy warm.

Greg Willson

www.ingramcontent.com/pod-product-compliance
Lightning Source LLC
Chambersburg PA
CBHW070437010526
44118CB00014B/2085